ROBOTS AND ANDROIDS

BY JOHN HAMILTON

Visit us at

www.abdopublishing.com

Published by ABDO Publishing Company, 4940 Viking Drive, Suite 622, Edina, Minnesota 55435.
Copyright ©2007 by Abdo Consulting Group, Inc. International copyrights reserved in all countries.
No part of this book may be reproduced in any form without written permission from the publisher.
ABDO & Daughters™ is a trademark and logo of ABDO Publishing Company.

Printed in the United States.

Editor: Paul Joseph
Graphic Design: John Hamilton
Cover Design: Neil Klinepier
Cover Illustration: *Big Sun of Mercury* ©1977 Don Maitz
Interior Photos and Illustrations: p 1 *Cosmic Rape* ©1979 Don Maitz; p 4 cover of *Astounding Science
Fiction*, Mary Evans Picture Library; p 5 *Silver Metal Lover* ©1981 Don Maitz; p 6 *Space Series A* ©1981
Don Maitz; p 7 Data, Getty Images; p 8 scene from *R.U.R.*, Corbis; p 9 *This Year's Model* ©1978 Don
Maitz; p 10 scene from *I, Robot*, Corbis; p 11 Isaac Asimov, Getty Images; p 12 running robot, Corbis;
p 13 scene from *I, Robot*, courtesy Twentieth Century Fox; p 14 cover of *I, Robot*, courtesy Bantam
Spectra; p 15 scene from *I, Robot*, Corbis; p 16 Borg Queen, Getty Images; p 17 *Spray Can Man* ©1982
Don Maitz; p 18 HAL 9000, courtesy MGM; p 19 (top and bottom) scenes from *The Matrix*, courtesy
Warner Bros. Pictures; p 20 cover of *Prey*, courtesy HarperCollins; p 21 nanobots and blood cells, Corbis;
p 22 TALON robot, U.S. Army; p 23 (top) Mars rover, NASA; p 23 (bottom) ballroom dancing robots,
Getty Images; p 24 scene from Metropolis, Getty Images; p 25 *Big Sun of Mercury* ©1977 Don Maitz;
p 26 Terminator, Getty Images; p 27 cover of *Fantastic Adventures*, Mary Evans Picture Library; p 28 (top
left) R2-D2 and C-3PO, Getty Images; p 28 (top right) Robot B-9, Corbis; p 28 (lower left) Marvin
the paranoid android, courtesy BBC Two; p 28 (lower right) Gort, Getty Images; p 29 (top left) Bender,
courtesy Fox Network; p 29 (top right) Iron Giant, courtesy Warner Bros. Pictures; p 29 (lower left)
Robby the Robot, courtesy MGM; p 29 (middle right) The Terminator, Getty Images; p 29 (lower right)
False Maria, courtesy Paramount Pictures; p 30 *The Phantom Creeps,* courtesy Universal Pictures.

Library of Congress Cataloging-in-Publication Data

Hamilton, John
  Robots and androids / John Hamilton.
    p. cm. -- (The world of science fiction)
  Includes index.
  ISBN-13: 978-1-59679-993-6
  ISBN-10: 1-59679-993-5
  1. Robotics--Juvenile literature. I. Title. II. Series.

TJ211.H25 2007
629.8'92--dc22

                    2006002764

CONTENTS

DOMO ARIGATO, MR. ROBOTO

Facing page: Silver Metal Lover, by Don Maitz. *Below:* The cover of the December, 1947, issue of *Astounding Science Fiction.*

One of the goals of science fiction, other than sheer, pulse-pounding adventure, is to examine our society. Through the lens of science fiction, we explore our hopes and fears for the future. One of the most common themes in sci fi is the impact of technology on humankind. Will computers and robots someday become so advanced that they develop wills of their own, with feelings and emotions? Would they have souls? And what if they turned against their creators, like mechanical Frankenstein monsters? Can humans survive such a robot uprising?

Artificial people have populated stories for centuries, even before science fiction was recognized as a genre of literature.

In ancient Norse mythology, the troll Hrungnir fought Thor, the God of Thunder, with the aid of a giant man made of clay called Mökkurkálfi, or Mistcalf. Hephaestus, the deformed Greek god of fire and patron of all craftsmen, created golden mechanical maids, plus three-legged tables that could walk around under their own power. In 1495, Leonardo Da Vinci made detailed drawings of a mechanical knight that could move its head, sit up, and wave its arms. It's doubtful that he tried to build this primitive robot, but the drawings exist in notebooks discovered in the 1950s.

In the world of science fiction, robots are mechanical persons or animals. They're usually made of a collection of electro-magnetic motors and mechanical parts. These allow robots to move around and manipulate their environment. Robots use high-tech cameras, microphones, and speakers to "see" and "speak." They are run by sophisticated computers that can evaluate the world around them and make decisions without direct human guidance.

Robots perform tasks that are either too dangerous or too boring for people in future societies. They take orders from the humans they replace. If you're a spaceship captain and the outside of your hull is damaged, why send a valuable crewman out to perform the risky repair? Instead, send a handy repair-bot. The machine doesn't mind the hard, cold vacuum of space, and it's unaffected by any radiation it might encounter.

A robot doesn't necessarily look like a human being. The repair-bot in the above example might perform more efficiently if it resembled a spider with suction-cup legs. *Androids*, on the

Below: Space Series A, by Don Maitz.

other hand, are specifically designed to mimic people. They are robots that resemble people in both appearance and behavior, as much as possible with the technology available. The word *droid,* from the *Star Wars* universe, is taken from the word android. In Douglas Adams' sci fi series, *The Hitchhiker's Guide to the Galaxy,* an android is referred to as "your plastic pal who's fun to be with."

In most science fiction tales, androids usually have quirks that separate them from true humans. Even the most sophisticated androids betray their robotic roots. Sometimes their skin doesn't look quite right, or they move too stiffly, or their emotions aren't fully developed. Data, the advanced android from *Star Trek: The Next Generation,* was constantly striving to learn what it meant to be a true human.

Left: Data, the android from *Star Trek: The Next Generation.*

Robots and androids are designed to help or even replace human beings. But should worker machines really replace people? It seems logical to create robots to do work that is dangerous, or boring. On the other hand, what about the people who are being replaced? How will they find new work? This debate is surprisingly old, dating back to the dawn of the Industrial Revolution of the 18ᵗʰ century, when factories and automation began replacing agriculture as a way of life.

In 1920, Czech playwright Karel Capek wrote a play called *R.U.R.*, which stands for "Rossum's Universal Robots." The term robot comes from the Czech word *robota*, which means "forced labor," or "servitude." In the play, robots are artificial humans put to work in factories. Their owners exploit and abuse them so much that the robots finally revolt and slaughter the human race.

Capek's suspenseful play was very popular. It was a time when people were thinking about the changing role of technology. Many people feared that mankind was growing too dependent on machines. They worried that mechanical humanoids might someday develop consciousness. The slaves would then turn the table on human beings, wiping them away to make room for a new robot civilization. It's a fear that continues today, as technology becomes ever more complex. We depend on computers and technology for so much today. How will weak and puny humans ever survive a robot uprising? Will we become extinct, victims of our own technology? Will robots someday inherit the earth? It's a theme that science fiction continues to explore.

Right: A scene from *R.U.R.*, a television production based on the play by Karel Capek. *Facing page: This Year's Model,* by Don Maitz.

I, ROBOT

Isaac Asimov was born on January 2, 1920, in Russia. After immigrating to the United States with his parents in 1923, he was writing stories by the time he was 11 years old. He went on to become one of the greatest science fiction authors of all time. He died in 1992, after penning more than 500 books, plus countless articles and essays.

One of Asimov's favorite science fiction subjects was robots. In the 1920s and 1930s, many science fiction stories were about robot slaves who revolted against their creators and went on killing sprees. Asimov grew tired of these stories. He set out to create a world where robots and humans could coexist peacefully. To Asimov, this was a more realistic and rational vision of the future.

Facing page: Isaac Asimov loved to write about robots. *Below:* A scene from *I, Robot*, the 2004 film starring Will Smith.

Asimov is most famous for his creation of the Three Laws of Robotics, which tell how robots should behave. Asimov imagined that each robot had a central computer called a "positronic brain," which was programmed to mimic human consciousness. Certain rules, called the Three Laws, were also programmed into the brains. Without these rules, the robot could not function. The Laws made sure that robots couldn't turn against their human masters, like mechanical Frankensteins. Asimov's point was to show that human lives could be made better through a mastery of our own technology.

ASIMOV'S THREE LAWS OF ROBOTICS:

1. A robot may not injure a human being, or, through inaction, allow a human being to come to harm.

2. A robot must obey the orders given it by human beings except where such orders would conflict with the First Law.

3. A robot must protect its own existence as long as such protection does not conflict with the First or Second Law.

The Three Laws didn't appear in Asimov's first two robot stories, *Robbie* and *Reason*. In *Robbie*, the Three Laws are hinted at when Robbie's human owner says, "He can't help being faithful, loving, and kind. He's a machine—made so." The first story to state all three Laws was *Runaround*, first published in 1942.

I, Robot is a collection of nine related robot stories written in the 1940s and 1950s. *Robbie,* the first, is a story about a mute RB-Series robot placed with a family to be a nursemaid for the couple's daughter. The little girl becomes very fond of Robbie, but the mother distrusts robots. She thinks Robbie is unsafe and dangerous. Her opinion about robots is later changed when Robbie saves the daughter from a potentially fatal accident.

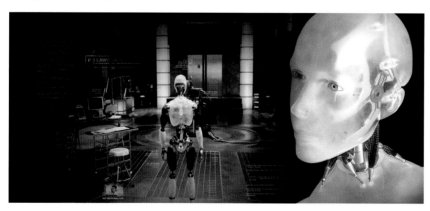

Left: A scene from the film, *I, Robot.* *Facing page:* A robot runs through a futuristic cityscape.

AUTHOR OF THE FOUNDATION NOVELS

ISAAC

ASIMOV

THE ROBOT SERIES

I, ROBOT

Above: A book cover of Isaac Asimov's *I, Robot.* *Facing page:* Will Smith gets some help from a robotic friend in this scene from the film, *I, Robot.*

Other authors have used Asimov's idea in their own stories. The Three Laws became so well known that they are somewhat overused today. Many science fiction stories include robots supposedly incapable of harming humans because of their programming. It's almost as if newer writers believe there really are laws governing robot behavior.

Besides its larger theme, Asimov used the Three Laws as a literary device, a kind of writing tool, which sets up mysteries within his robot stories. One of Asimov's recurring characters is Dr. Susan Calvin. She is a robot psychologist who comes to love the steel fellows. She once said, "To you, a robot is just a robot. But you haven't worked with them. You don't know them. They're a cleaner, better breed than we are."

When a robot malfunctions, Dr. Calvin is often called on to investigate. For example, in 1941's *Liar!*, Dr. Calvin examines the case of a robot, RB-34 (Herbie), created with the ability to read minds. Herbie begins lying to his human masters after reading their thoughts. Dr. Calvin discovers that he is doing this because he doesn't want to hurt his masters' feelings. But in lying, he is hurting them anyway, and violating Rule Number One: "a robot may not injure a human being."

As each story's mystery unfolds, the fault is almost never with the robots. Instead, imperfect and illogical humans are mostly to blame. In Isaac Asimov's creative world, robots are just like you and me. By studying robots, we can learn about ourselves, and what rules we should live by. Robots are an example of the best, and sometimes the worst, of what it means to be human.

15

CYBORGS

A *cyborg* is a being that is part human, part machine. It might be a human with mechanical limbs, or perhaps a computer chip is installed in a person's brain to help him think faster. Science fiction author Edmond Hamilton used the idea of cyborgs in several of his short stories. His *Captain Future* series included an old and diseased scientist whose brain was transplanted into a hovering, artificial case from which he could continue to communicate and work.

The Six Million Dollar Man featured astronaut Steve Austin, who survived a terrible crash and was rebuilt with robotic legs, right arm, and left eye. Austin was also called the "bionic man," which is another term for a cyborg. This robotic assistance gave him superhuman powers, which he used in his work as a secret agent.

In the 1987 film *Robocop*, a police officer is mutilated on the job. Surgeons save him by grafting what remained of his body into a nearly impervious titanium outer shell, complete with thermal vision and a machine-pistol stored in a retractable holster in his right thigh.

Star Trek's Borg are alien humanoid cyborgs. They are a tough, warlike collection of races who survive the rigors of space travel by using cybernetic implants. Their implanted computer modules and robot-assisted limbs make them able to adapt to almost any situation.

Facing page: Spray Can Man, by Don Maitz.
Below: The Borg Queen threatens Captain Janeway in a scene from *Star Trek: Voyager.*

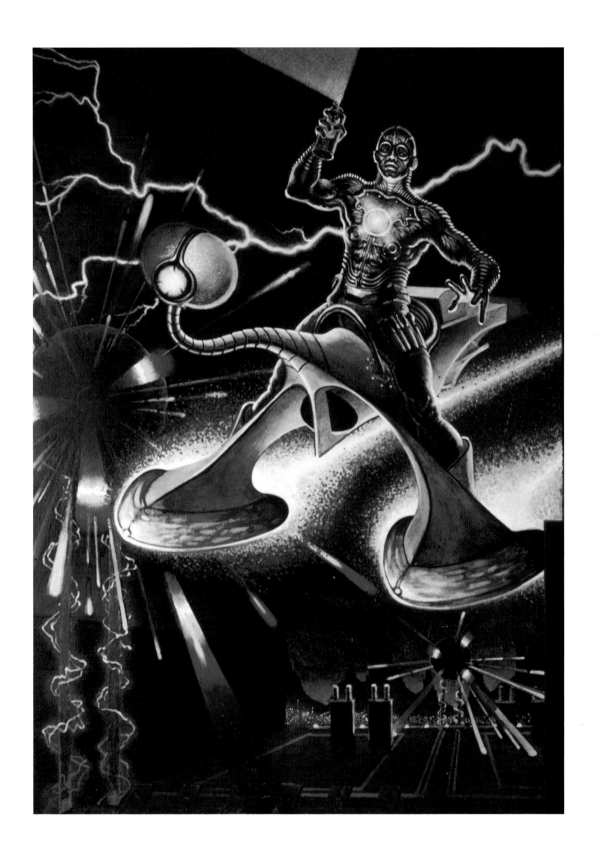

ARTIFICIAL INTELLIGENCE

AI stands for Artificial Intelligence. It is the science of trying to make computers that can solve problems and achieve goals as well as, or better than, human beings. In science fiction, computers that achieve AI usually begin acting in unexpected ways, sometimes harming people. There are many sci fi stories of advanced computers turning on their masters by manipulating their environment, including reprogramming robots to carry out their schemes.

In some stories, robots themselves achieve artificial intelligence, and human masters must learn to cope with their newly created mechanical life forms. In *Artificial Intelligence: AI*, the 2001 film directed by Steven Spielberg, David is a robot, or mecha, who is abandoned by his human mother. David goes on a quest to become a real boy so that his mother will take him back and love him once more. It's a heartbreaking story with no real happy ending.

In Stanley Kubrick's 1968 film, *2001: A Space Odyssey* (written by science fiction great Arthur C. Clarke), a highly advanced computer called HAL 9000 controls a spaceship with a crew trying to make contact with an unknown alien civilization. HAL isn't technically a robot, but he guides the spaceship. In effect, the ship is his body.

Below: The menacing "eye" of HAL 9000, the malfunctioning computer of *2001: A Space Odyssey.*

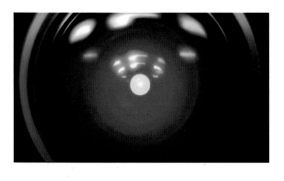

During the voyage, HAL makes a technical mistake, even though he is supposed to be "perfect." Suspecting a major malfunction, the disturbed astronauts consider disconnecting the computer. To protect himself, HAL proceeds to murder the crew, until the last remaining astronaut manages to shut down HAL's central data banks.

The Matrix is a frightening 1999 film about intelligent machines that enslave humans and use their bodies unwittingly as a power source. The AI computers make use of robots in their war against humanity. The enslaved humans are fooled because they live in a computer-generated illusion called the "Matrix," a simulated reality in which the humans have no knowledge of the war between people and computers. In reality, they live in cocoon-like vats of liquid. The heat and electricity generated by their bodies is harvested by the machines. To keep them under control, the human slaves have their brains directly connected to the AI computers, which control how people perceive and experience reality. Inside the Matrix, people lead regular, everyday life. In "the real world," the human race is trapped in a nightmare.

Above: Neo, played by Keanu Reeves, stops bullets by manipulating the Matrix with his mind.
Below: Neo is freed from his machine-controlled cocoon in this scene from *The Matrix.*

Groups of freedom fighters manage to unplug their brains from the Matrix so they can fight against the AI machines. They are led by Neo, a man who can alter computer code with his mind. *The Matrix* spawned two sequels, *The Matrix Reloaded* and *The Matrix Revolutions*, both released in 2003.

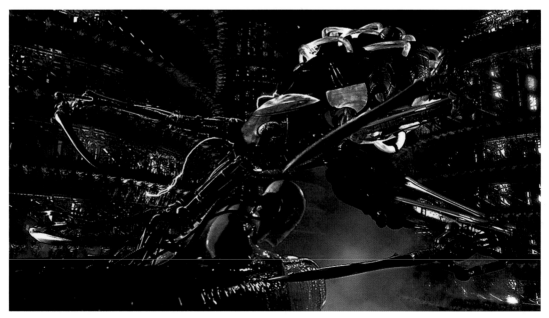

NANOBOTS

Some robots are so small that you have to use a microscope to see them. Nanotechnology is the science of building tiny machines called nanomachines, or nanobots. Work is progressing rapidly on producing nanobots with tiny gears and joints, and protruding arms that can manipulate objects.

Nanobots are very, very small, less than 100 nanometers in size. One nanometer is one billionth of a meter. The width of a human hair, by comparison, is about 100 microns. (A micron is 1,000 nanometers.) That means you could line up about 1,000 nanobots and they would be about the same width as a strand of hair.

Nanobots are a very new technology. Simple nanomachines are used today to make computers faster and more powerful, to make clothing more stain-resistant, or to make high-performance sunscreen lotion. But future applications of true nanobots might include tiny machines swimming in people's bloodstreams that zap harmful cholesterol deposits, or self-replicating machines that create layers of artificial diamonds on our roads to make them almost maintenance free.

Sometimes it seems as if science is developing faster than our ability to control the results. That fear has fueled several science fiction stories about nanotechnology in recent years.

In Michael Crichton's 2002 novel, *Prey*, a swarm of microscopic machines escapes from a top-secret desert laboratory used by the military. Without central control by humans, the self-replicating nanobots adjust to their environment. They begin feeding on mammals, including humans. The nanobots then attack the laboratory. The out-of-control machines seem intent on killing the scientists trapped inside. It's a frightening story about the dangers of new technology that we can't control or don't fully understand.

Facing page: Nanobots travel amidst red blood cells, cleaning up viruses.
Below: The cover of Michael Crichton's techno-thriller, *Prey.*

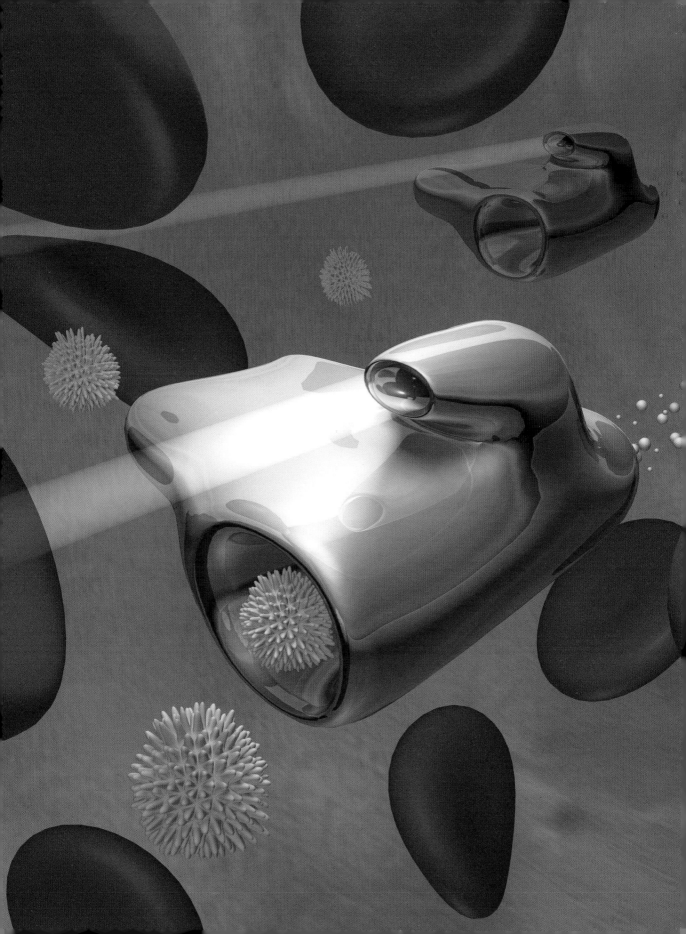

ROBOTS TODAY

Robots are so common today that sometimes it seems we hardly even notice them. They have been used in the automotive industry for many years, taking the place of human workers to perform dangerous or boring tasks such as welding or painting. Industrial robots are used to automate many other tasks, including replacing radioactive fuel rods at nuclear power plants.

The military and many police forces use robots to dispose of bombs, or to enter buildings where an enemy might be hiding. An "explosive ordnance disposal" (EOD) robot called "TALON" is used by the U.S. Army in Iraq and Afghanistan to safely dispose of bombs. It can also be used to search for the enemy, and can be fitted with machine guns to enter a fight. Controlled by a remote operator with a joystick, TALON robots are fast, can climb stairs, and weigh less than 100 pounds (45 kg). They are very tough. In Iraq, an explosion blew a TALON robot off a military vehicle crossing a bridge and plunged into a river. Soldiers were able to use the robot's control unit to drive it out of the water onto the shore, where it was retrieved.

Below: A U.S. Army TALON explosive ordnance disposal robot used in Baghdad, Iraq.

Robots today are not limited to crawling around on the ground. Predator unmanned drones are used by the U.S. Air Force to fly over hostile territory. They were originally used to spy on the enemy, but can now be fitted with AGM-114 Hellfire missiles, which can destroy armored targets such as tanks or bunkers. Predators are about 29 feet (9 m) long, with a wingspan of about 49 feet (15 m). They have been used successfully in Iraq, Afghanistan, Pakistan, and Bosnia.

Left: A computer graphic of the *Spirit* rover on the surface of Mars.

NASA makes extensive use of robots in space. The *Spirit* and *Opportunity* rovers have been exploring the harsh, forbidding surface of Mars since January 2004. As of this writing, the rovers have lasted more than two years, much longer than their original mission of 90 days.

Robots are also created today simply for fun, or as experiments for the future. In 2005, a Japanese researcher invented the world's first ballroom-dancing robot. With a female face and a bright pink gown, the machine matches the movements of its human dance partner.

Below: A man dances with the Partner Ballroom Dance Robots (PBDR) at the Prototype Robot Exhibition in Nagakute, Japan.

RISE OF THE MACHINES

Through his stories and novels, Isaac Asimov tried to improve the bad image of robots. Despite Asimov's best efforts, most robots in science fiction today are viewed suspiciously as potential monsters.

In some science fiction tales, however, especially in movies, robots do obey their programming and behave themselves. Robby the Robot, from the 1956 film *Forbidden Planet*, along with the similarly shaped bubble-headed Robot B-9 from the 1960s TV series *Lost in Space*, were helpful and eager to please. B-9 always kept a watchful eye on the youngest member of the marooned Robinson family. Whenever an intruder threatened, B-9 was quick to sound the alarm, "Danger! Danger, Will Robinson!" In the *Star Wars* movies, C-3PO and R2-D2 are helpful, even heroic.

But for every nice robot, there is a mechanical menace lurking in the shadows. It's a common fear that mankind's technology will someday turn against us. In 1926, Fritz Lang directed *Metropolis*, in which an insane inventor creates an evil robot named Maria. In 1976's *Futureworld*, a group of robots plot to replace humans and take over the world.

Right: A scene from Fritz Lang's *Metropolis*. *Facing page: Big Sun of Mercury*, by Don Maitz.

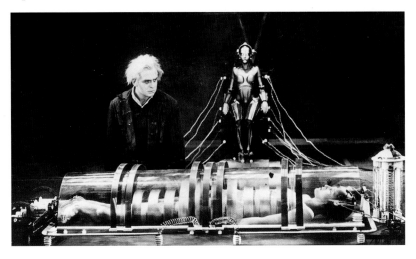

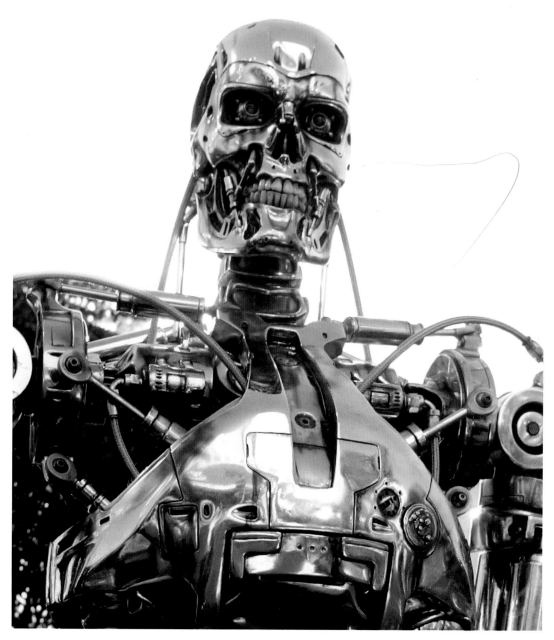

Above: The murderous robot from James Cameron's 1984 film, *The Terminator.*

More graphic examples of robots-run-amok include *The Terminator*, directed by James Cameron in 1984. Arnold Schwarzenegger plays an unstoppable cyborg assassin, sent from the future to kill the mother of a human rebel leader. And in 1984's *Alien*, Ash is another human-looking robot who holds a dark secret.

In 1982, Ridley Scott directed *Blade Runner*. The plot was taken from the mind-bending novel written by science fiction author Philip K. Dick, called *Do Androids Dream of Electric Sheep?*

Blade Runner became one of the most influential science fiction films of all time. It tells the story of Rick Deckard. He is a member of a special police force called Blade Runners, who hunt down and kill human-looking androids called "replicants." The world of *Blade Runner* is bleak and depressing, a frightening vision of the future. The film helped spawn the modern science fiction sub-genre of cyberpunk.

In *Blade Runner*, a group of escaped replicants (sometimes called "skin jobs" by insensitive humans) have received advanced programming to make them seem even more human. But on Earth, they are still seen as a menace. Deckard is called in to hunt them down. Before their time runs out, the replicants try to contact their creator in an attempt to prolong their short lives.

In this conversation between Deckard and Eldon Tyrell, the head of the company that manufactures replicants, Tyrell explains how his androids are made so life-like:

Tyrell: "More human than human is our motto… We began to recognize in them a strange obsession. After all, they are emotionally inexperienced with only a few years in which to store up the experiences which you and I take for granted. If we give them a past, we create a cushion or pillow for their emotions, and consequently we can control them better."

Deckard: "Memories. You're talking about memories."

As with all good science fiction, *Blade Runner* holds a mirror up to ourselves and makes us think. What does it mean to be human? Is it ethical to make a machine so human-like, and then deny it freedom? As Deckard wrestles with these questions, we see how precious all life can be, and how much it should be treasured.

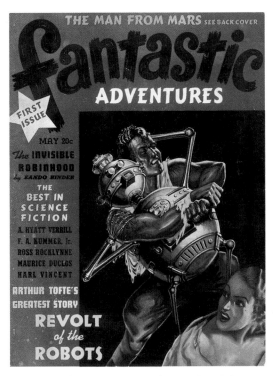

Above: The debut issue of *Fantastic Adventures*, featuring Arthur Tofte's "Revolt of the Robots."

TEN GREAT ROBOTS
OF SCIENCE FICTION

R2-D2 AND **C-3PO**
STAR WARS—1977

ROBOT B-9
LOST IN SPACE—1965-1968

MARVIN THE **PARANOID ANDROID**
THE HITCHHIKER'S GUIDE TO THE GALAXY—1981

GORT
THE DAY THE EARTH STOOD STILL—1951

BENDER
FUTURAMA—1999-2003

THE GIANT
THE IRON GIANT—1999

ROBBY THE ROBOT
FORBIDDEN PLANET—1956

T-800
THE TERMINATOR—1984

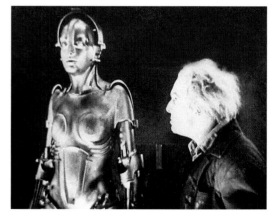

FALSE MARIA
METROPOLIS—1927

GLOSSARY

ANDROID
A kind of robot that mimics people, both in appearance and behavior. In the film *Blade Runner*, based on Philip K. Dick's *Do Androids Dream of Electric Sheep?*, replicants are a type of android.

A robot attacks in 1939's *The Phantom Creeps.*

ARTIFICIAL INTELLIGENCE
A computer that is so advanced that it mimics human thought. Also referred to as AI.

CYBERNETICS
The science of control and communication of both machines and living creatures.

CYBERPUNK
The word cyberpunk is a combination of the words punk and cybernetics. Originally, it was meant to describe antisocial rebels who use computers to commit their crimes. Nowadays, cyberpunk more commonly refers to a tech-savvy hero who fights back, using the system against itself.

CYBORG
A being that is part human and part machine. Steve Austin (*The Six Million Dollar Man*), Robocop, and *Star Trek's* Borg are all cyborgs.

GALAXY
A system of millions, or even hundreds of billions, of stars and planets, clustered together in a distinct shape, like a spiral or ellipse. Our Earth is located within the Milky Way Galaxy.

GENRE
A type, or kind, or a work of art. In literature, a genre is distinguished by a common subject, theme, or style. Some genres include science fiction, fantasy, and mystery.

HUMANOID
Looking like or behaving like a human being. A humanoid alien would typically have a torso, four limbs, and a head.

INDUSTRIAL REVOLUTION
The rapid development of industry that happened in the late 18th and early 19th centuries, especially in Great Britain and other Western countries. The Industrial Revolution is usually characterized by steam power, the growth of factories, and mass-manufactured goods. Science fiction became popular as science and manufacturing became more and more important in people's lives.

NASA
The National Aeronautics and Space Administration. NASA is the United States' main space agency, responsible for programs such as the Space Shuttle and unmanned space probes.

NORSE
The people, language, or culture of Scandinavia, especially medieval Scandinavia. The Vikings were famous Nordic people.

INDEX